CÓRDOBA

RICARDO MOLINA

CÓRDOBA

EDITORIAL NOGUER, S. A. BARCELONA

ENGLISH TRANSLATION BY
JOHN FORRESTER

PHOTOGRAPHS BY
EUGEN HAAS, ANDERSON, TEJADA, ARCHIVO MAS,
RUIZ VERNACCI, CAMPAÑÁ-PUIG FERRÁN AND TORMO

COLOUR PHOTO
PAUL PIETZSCH

3rd. EDITION: 1960

DEPÓSITO LEGAL B. 4730 - 1960

Rotogravure: Heraclio Fournier, S. A. - Vitoria
Text printed by Imprenta Vélez, Travesera de Dalt, 44 - Barcelona

THE FACE OF CÓRDOBA

In Córdoba we have a fine modern city, blessed with all the comforts and amenities of present day life, situated some 100-150 metres above sea level, at the foot of the loveliest of all Andalusian mountain ranges and washed by the Guadalquivir, "King of deep flowing rivers"; but to this rich and prominent modern aspect of her life you must add her past, still living and dominant, which illumines her with strange, glowing shafts of light.

If we admit the traditional supposition of her having originated as a Phoenician colony, Córdoba must have already been an important urban centre in the VIIIth and VIIth Centuries B. C. (according to some historians she was the Turdetan capital). Her rich mines, the prehistoric remains and the Iberian idols since discovered all go to confirm the hypothesis that Córdoba was contemporary with Tartesus.

Córdoba enjoyed the privilege of an Immune Patrician Colony in Roman Spain, receiving the rank of capital of Outer Spain during the first centuries of Latin domination. And it is that patrician Roman Córdoba which has given its nobly imperial shape and form to the Córdoba of today. Both the material and moral links binding the city are Roman; the accumulated wisdom of the City of the Seven Hills has left its mark on local history and Cordobese culture through the course of twenty-two centuries. A Roman influence can be traced in both the character

5

and the works of illustrious Cordobese, from Mena[1] down to Lagartijo[2].

The Spanish-Moslem Empire raised Córdoba to such heights as could only be compared to those achieved by Byzantium, Baghdad, classical Athens or XIXth Century Paris. Then was she the "ornament of the world", illuminating the Occident with her science and powerful influence. The marked presence of Córdoba in gothic art, and in scholastic sciences and philosophy is an unquestionable fact.

Reconquered from the Moslems by San Fernando in 1236, and afterwards the favourite residence of many Castilian sovereigns (Alfonso XI, Pedro I and the Catholic Sovereigns). Córdoba lived on her splendid patrician and caliphal tradition during the XVIth, XVIIth, XVIIIth and XIXth Centuries; she continued to leave the mark of her influence on all the most important political and spiritual events of these epochs. Alonso de Quesada, founder of Santa Fe de Bogotá, the Viceroy Caballero Góngora[3], Gonzalo Fernández de Córdoba[4], don Luis Carrillo Sotomayor[5], Céspedes[6], don Luis de Góngora[7], and don Ángel Saavedra, Duque de Rivas[8], are the outstanding figures produced by her in these centuries. Córdoba, materially speaking a dead city since the XIth Century, devastated by numerous invasions and local political upheavals, continued to breathe only through such men, and through them continues to exercise her power over the spirit, for she is essentially a spiritual city.

At the present time Córdoba is passing through a phase of renovation and growth; fortunately, such modern additions and improvements have not in any way affected the old traditional city — side by side with modern Córdoba, a city of noble buildings and spacious avenues, the old Córdoba, "Roman and Moorish", as Machado[9] said, still lives. Lorca[10] wrote of her as being "distant and remote".

---

[1] Juan de Mena, author of a famous work, *Laberinto de Fortuna* (1411-1456). [2] Rafael Molina, *Lagartijo;* a renowned torero (1841-1900). [3] An XVIIIth Century Spanish prelate, who was archbishop and Viceroy of New Granada. [4] A great Spanish General, known as *El Gran Capitán* (1453-1515). [5] Luis Carrillo de Sotomayor, a notable poet (1583-1610). [6] Pablo de Céspedes, painter and poet (1538-1603). [7] Luis de Góngora y Argote, one of the greatest of Spanish poets (1561-1627). [8] Ángel de Saavedra y Ramírez de Baquedano, Duque de Rivas, one of the outstanding poets of the Romantic era (1791-1865). [9] Antonio Machado, a great Spanish poet (1875-1939). [10] Federico García Lorca, an important contemporany poet (1898-1936).

6

Córdoba is one of the grand monumental cities of Spain; you would be hard put to it to find another place where every little corner, every street and every patio in the private houses can display such artistry before your eyes in so great a profusion and yet so naturally; here is one city that has known how to turn its back on those superfluities of adornment which in the end serve only to tire and bore the visitor.

Here is the very Queen of the Andalusian style of constructing patios; in no other spot will you find so many, nor such beautiful ones as in this superb city smothered in night scented stock, rambling roses sweet basil, palms and orange trees...

Córdoba is a city of hidden streets and squares, sunk in the fragrant aroma of lemon trees and lost in the silence of centuries; streets which reflect a white or golden glow from the lime or ochre washed houses, clean and pleasant smelling streets, the play of sun and shadow making violent contrasts of light and shade.

This city of Córdoba is the centre of the *cante hondo*[1]; in the whole of Andalusia only Jerez de la Frontera can approach the old Moorish capital in this sphere of music; here we have the real *cante hondo*, with none of the outside infiltrations and additions: the *soleá*, the *serrana*, the *fandango campiñero* and the *alegría de Córdoba*; the *seguiriya*, the *polo*, and the *caña*[2] are found here on their native ground.

The Cordobese himself is of a quiet, reflective turn of mind, with a trace of Oriental nonchalance and Roman aplomb; the atmosphere of peacefulness of spirit and age-old tradition has had its leavening effect upon the soul of the people. The typical citizen of Córdoba is measured in his speech and has a natural elegance of manner; he is hospitable, though without any showiness, and proverbially discreet. If you should happen to pause for a moment at the door of his house or on the threshold of his patio, he will ask you to enter, with a gracious smile. Ask him for a certain street or a monument and he will at once accompany you there himself, pointing out to you on the way all the things he thinks you ought to notice. Amongst the Cordobese you will feel at

---

[1] *Cante hondo* is a style of Andalusian singing which is very notable, and can possibly be attributed to Arab origins. The songs are sung by a soloist, the *cantaor,* accompanied by a guitarist. *Cante flamenco* is often used synonymously with *cante hondo,* although the former is another style of singing, derived *from cante hondo* but inferior in quality and purity.   [2] Varieties of *cante hondo.*

home immediately, and nobody can better them at improvising an itinerary of artistic interest for you, or the unforgettable magic of a recital of singing and dancing in the patio or the garden of one of those inns that are so hidden away one would be inclined to say they seem to be submerged in an almost conventual calm. A tavern is here something so delightfully clean and so characteristically Cordobese that you must not for one instant think you can hope to appreciate the spirit of Córdoba without having visited a number of them and breathed their own particular atmosphere. This is a city where the taverns have an ageless charm and mellowness, like the superb wine they dispense; you can go into of them, sure of finding an exquisite drink, pleasant company and good manners.

CÓRDOBA AND THE MOSQUE

Córdoba and its Mosque have so often been identified together in a particular way that many people have the idea that once the latter edifice has been visited there is no valid reason to prolong one's stay in the city. Of course, compared with the Mosque, all other buildings are but shadows, but the same thing happens in other cities, without in any way detracting artistic value and interest from less grandiose and characteristic structures. Away from the immediate surroundings of the Mosque there is much that is well worth seeing; Córdoba itself, the city of silent streets and hidden squares, of tucked away *compases* [1], hushed by the soft lullaby of a sparkling fountain; of winding streets, where moss grows between the cracks in the paving stones, and the whole city wrapped in a peacefulness akin to that of some tiny village. The impression gained as a whole however is so profoundly stirring that it forms a balance to the emotions awakened by the Arabic marvel of the Mosque.

For this reason you must not be satisfied with a visit to the Mosque if you want to come to know Córdoba; the city is the living frame surrounding this great monument and the two cannot be separated. You must see all of Córdoba. Yet it is so difficult for us to map out an itinerary. A more or less fixed plan is required for cities where things of artistic merit, or otherwise

---

[1] *Compás* is a patio situated between the street and the house.

8

interesting, are the exception rather than the rule, but in Córdoba, where at every step and turn one is faced with yet another example of the creative spirit that has moved its people throughout the centuries, it would be far better for you simply to follow your fancy whither it led you through the streets, the better to be able to contemplate each new object of beauty as it came before your eyes.

All the same, we recognise the difficulties besetting a visitor who is left to discover a city in such a happy-go-lucky way, especially when it is such a city as Córdoba and we shall draw up, not a rigid itinerary, but rather a sensible way of calling the visitor's attention, so that nothing is lost.

I. THE MOSQUE AND ITS SURROUNDINGS

As a mark of aesthetic and archeological courtesy we must make our first visit that of the Mosque-Cathedral, taking as a starting point *plaza de José Antonio,* the centre of the modern city, which will only serve to deepen the impression the great Arab monument is sure to have on us. Yet, even here in *plaza de José Antonio* we are reminded of the city's past by the splendid equestrian statue of the *Gran Capitán,* Gonzalo Fernández de Córdoba, the work being a creation of Mateo Inurria.

Once past *calle del Duque de Hornachuelos* we have a very tranquil square, *plaza de la Compañía,* enclosed by the parish church of the Saviour *(El Salvador)* and the *Pórtico* of the *Colegiata de Santa Victoria;* in the middle of the square four columns form one of many *Triunfos de Rafael,* the Guardian Archangel of Córdoba.

In the CHURCH OF EL SALVADOR you can admire a rich churrigueresque retable, bearing a number of sculptures by Pedro Duque Cornejo, whose greatest masterpiece is the choir stalls in our cathedral.

The staircase of the former COLLEGE OF THE COMPANY OF JESUS (Jesuits), today a college of the *Maristas,* is a striking example of the rich Andalusian baroque style. Both the church of *El Sal-*

vador and the Graeco-Roman doorway of the COLEGIATA DE SANTA VICTORIA were built in the XVIIth Century.

What a distance one traverses in spirit between *plaza de José Antonio* and the calmly serene place that is *plaza de la Compañía!* The noise and the frenzied bustle of modern life here have completely vanished and surrendered their influence to a peace and tranquility typified by the six columns which form Santa Victoria. A long balcony facing the *Colegio de la Compañía* displays the rich colours of its hanging garden, and the blue skies or the starry night create a dome over this peaceful corner, so near the urban centre whose air is shattered into fragments by the constant rush of traffic.

Going along the narrow little alleyway that is *callejita de Angel de Saavedra* we come face to face with the old house which belonged to the MARQUESES DE FUENSANTA DEL VALLE — today the Conservatory of Music and Declamation — where the entrance is typical of the fusion between gothic and plateresque styles of architecture. We continue along *calle Blanco Belmonte,* where the house of the FERNÁNDEZ DE MESA family gives rather a solemn note to the surroundings. In *calle Comedias* there is still a Moorish bath house, which can be seen through a grating from the street; the bathroom, with its columns supporting semi-circular arches and the vaulted roof is still preserved, and one can notice lighting shafts which were employed for the ventilation of the establishment. According to the novelist Zunzunegui, the abundant use of water was a luxury enjoyed by the Romans, but it was also something typically Arab-Cordobese. If we can believe Arab historians, more than 900 bathing establishments were opened for the Moslem population during the time of the Caliphate.

We must not forget to go along *calle de las Flores* as far as the tiny place at the end, full of Andalusian charm with its fountain and arch, a spot from where you can obtain a very original view of the Mosque.

Returning to *calle Comedias,* you come out facing the Altar of the VIRGEN DE LOS FAROLES; the retable, protected by a little roof and pretty fences, displays a picture by Romero de Torres which shows the Assumption of Our Lady. The *Virgen de los Faroles* (Virgin of the Lamps) is one of the traditional objects of devotion in the city, and even folkloric songs take up the theme, as in this couplet:

Al pasar el Caño Gordo,	On passing the Caño Gordo
le he rezao por mis amores	I prayed for my love
a esa Virgen tan gitana	To this gypsy Virgin
que hay rodeaíta de faroles.	Surrounded by lamps.

At last we find ourselves in front of the Mosque-Cathedral. An old yellow wall encloses the sacred rectangle. One might even say that the famous line by Góngora was written especially about this wall:

¡Oh, excelso muro, oh torres coronadas...!

Oh, wonderful wall, oh crowned towers... !

In this northern wall the majestic *Puerta del Perdón,* a superb example of arabesque decoration, opens on the *Sahn* or Patio of Orange Trees, a marvellous place whose only ornament is formed by the age-old orange trees and the graceful, slender palms, the two combining to lend a note of colour and shade to the scene. A number of little fountains scattered among the orange trees shoot their glittering streams towards the sun. To the east of this tower is the *Fuente del Caño del Olivo,* shaded by an ancient olive tree.

Notice how beautiful is this patio, yet how simple; its magic charm is drawn from Nature herself, without resource to artifice. Here is a garden whose sole elements are water and sunlight, stone and shadow. The quiet splendour of such a corner is in complete harmony with the Doric simplicity of Caliphal art, with the noble Latin-Cordobese tradition, and with the very character of the people.

The arches and columns of the east and west galleries harmoniously underline the ensemble. In these galleries, which are of the XVth Century construction although they were probably originally Moslem, there are still remains of the wonderful old craftsmanship employed. There are four doors, two on the east and two on the west, which break the walls to the exterior; the most remarkable of them are that of *Santa Catalina* in the east wall, and *Los Deanes* and *El postigo de la Leche* in the west wall.

With certain variations, they are all of the same type of horseshoe arch with the tympanum adorned with reliefs. Over the

11

door is a freize of blind arches and two lateral windows covered with blinds and inscriptions under horseshoe arches. This type of doorway is a reproduction of the *Portada de San Esteban* on the western wall, the only one to be conserved from the VIIIth Century. In general, the doorways restored in the XVth, XVIth and XVIIth Centuries show signs of the architectural features prevalent at the time: gothic, renaissance or baroque. On the other hand, those restored in the XIXth and XXth Centuries, under the guidance of the architect Velázquez Bosco, have attempted to reconstruct the original form and decorations.

From any angle of this patio you can contemplate the tower, a beautiful yet solid structure the colour of old wine; surmounting its cupola is an image of San Rafael, sculpted by Pedro de Paz in the XVIIth Century. At first sight we get the impression of a Herrerian style, but when we look more attentively we find a series of little balconies and other decorations that are pure baroque. The tower has undergone a number of changes in the course of eight centuries. It was originally a minaret in the time of Abderramán (Xth Century); then the architect, Hernán Ruiz (XVIth Century) built the present tower on the old minaret.

Entering the Mosque-Cathedral by either the *Puerta de Las Palmas* or that of *Las Bendiciones,* one is immediately confronted with the wonderful vista of the eleven naves erected by Abderrahman from 785 onwards; hardly have we crossed the threshold before we are aware of an atmosphere that is at once soft and flower-like and yet recalls the mysteries of a labyrinth — it is as though in contrast to the light-filled *Patio de los Naranjos* we have entered a secret, withdrawn oasis. The innumerable shafts of the columns of jasper, marble, and all manner of priceless stone stretch before us, surmounted by the fantastic variety of the capitals (romanesque, visigoth, arab), the whole made uniform by the superb arching, bordered alternately in red and yellow, interrupted here and there by the marvel of the Mihrab or the delicate workmanship of the chapel of Villaviciosa. The Mosque is bathed in a half-light that seems unreal and which inspires in us a feeling of silent contemplation or meditation. The nineteen grand and multicoloured naves offer a wonderful setting in which one feels lost, as in the depths of a forest. This, the most beautiful and spacious mosque in the world, is a living expression of the architectural vitality of the Cordobese caliphate of which the Mosque is the most representative example.

There was a visigoth cathedral in Córdoba, dedicated to San Vicente, but from 748 the Mozarabs were compelled to share it with the Moslems, so that two different creeds were thenceforward practised under the same roof — the same thing occurred in Syria and other countries — as each sect used half of the edifice. In 785, Abderrahman I finally dispossessed the Christians of their half of the basilica, in order to erect the Mosque on the same site; use was made of the primitive building in its construction, and work was finished in about twelve months. According to Arab historians, the earlier edifice was a sumptuous structure. The Moslem architects simply pulled down the five naves of the cathedral of San Vicente and reconstructed them according to their own ideas, changing their position and making use of the material already available. It is for this reason that the Mosque is extremely interesting for its visigoth remains.

For its sheer elegance and balance, the exterior arching surpasses anything done either before or since. Its combination of horseshoe arches linking the pillars, while others soar to the heights in semi-circular flights, constitutes an ensemble that appears to be the work of some magician. Further enlargements were made by Abderrahman II, Alhaquen II and Almanzor, each one further increasing the magnificence of this great monument; one such innovation was the lobed arch, Mesopotamian in origin, which can be seen and admired in all its splendour in the Mihrab arching, constructed during the reign of Alhaquen II. Of especial interest, from the decorative and architectural viewpoint is the typically Cordobese idea of covering a square space with polychromed domes of a dazzling richness, a procedure akin to that of adorning the walls of the Mihrab with magnificent Byzantine-Caliphal mosaics. This system of roofing can be most perfectly admired in the Mihrab or in the chapel of Villaviciosa; it marks a great technical and aesthetic advance in the art of the Caliphate, and no doubt was an outstanding example for the architects of the epoch, and of later times too, though Córdoba not only exercised a profound influence in the realm of architecture, but also in all other branches of culture. The Caliphate of Córdoba was at its apogee when such great progress was made, and the prominent intellectual figure of Alhaquen II was one of the personalities of his time; this wise ruler put together one of the most richly endowed libraries in the world, and was an enthusiastic patron of all the arts and sciences, but especially of architecture. Perhaps the highest praise that one can offer his memory is that the prodigious structure of the Mihrab, erected during his reign, might be said to be the swan song of Caliphal architecture.

From the Mihrab we go on the chapel of Villaviciosa, facing the former, yet another marvel of the artistry of the craftsmen of the Caliphate. From this chapel we make our way to the main chapel, or Christian cathedral, set in the very heart of the Mosque; finely proportioned, gracious, and filled with light, it was built in the XVIth Century, during the reign of Carlos V, who was later sorry that he had permitted its construction. It was begun in the renaissance style with traces of ogival influence, as can be seen by the line of the main arches, those of the chancel and those of the choir, but on the death of the architect, Hernán Ruiz, work was continued in the plateresque style (vaulted roof and windows). The choir back is markedly Graeco-Roman in form. The red marble main retable is adorned with paintings by Palomino, representing the Assumption of Mary, and Saints Acisclo, Victoria, Flora, and Pelagio; and sculptures of the Eternal Father, the Virtues, Saint Peter and Saint Paul, by Pedro Paz.

The huge silver lamp hanging in front of the retable is the work of a Cordobese silversmith, Martín Sánchez de la Cruz (1620). The churrigueresque pulpits, a superb piece of craftsmanship, were the creation of a French sculptor, Michel Verdiguier. The magnificent choir, one of the most beautiful in all Spain, was carried out by an XVIIIth Century Sevillian sculptor, Pedro Duque Cornejo.

This cathedral, set in the midst the Mosque, comes as something of a surprise to the visitor. Its striking contrast with the Arab building serves to point out yet more forcefully the aesthetic differences between the two religions and the two schools of artistry. Yet, we must pause a while, and think that since its very foundation this wonderful edifice was destined to shelter two distinct religious creeds under one roof.

Of the chain of Christian chapels surrounding the Mosque, in the west wall the most outstanding are; the chapel of *Nuestra Señora de la Concepción,* where three statues on the altar, the work of Pedro de Mena, are especially worthy of attention, and the chapel of *San Pedro y San Lorenzo,* where the roofing probably still retains authentic traces of the old Mosque. The ivory figure of Christ Crucified, on the left, is a work by Martínez Montañés.

In the south wall we should take particular note of: the chapel of *San Bartolomé,* where the very Prince of Spanish poets, don Luis de Góngora y Argote, sleeps in eternal rest, and the chapel of *Santa Teresa,* remarkable for a sculpture of the Santa Doctora, by José de Mora, three paintings by Palomino, and two beautiful carvings by Alonso Cano, representing the Assumption and the Conception. In an annex to this chapel is kept the Cathedral treasure amongst which stands out the marvellous Custody of Enrique de Arfe (1517). On the south wall, a splendid retable depicting the *Last Supper,* by Céspedes, can be contemplated and admired.

In the east wall our attention is especially drawn by the chapel of the Holy Spirit, the work of Hernán Ruiz, where, at Christ's feet, in the second part of the retable, we can see paintings by Pablo de Céspedes, as also in the chapel of *Santa Ana,* where the socles are by the famous Cordobese painter.

Of the chapels in the north wall, we would draw to your notice the chapel of *Nuestra Señora del Rosario,* where you can see paintings of Our Lady of the Rosary, and of San Roque and San Sebastián, by Antonio del Castillo; and the chapel of *San Esteban,* remarkable for its fine paintings by Juan Luis Zambrano.

On leaving through the *Puerta de los Deanes,* we find ourselves in the doorway of *San Jacinto,* facing the west wall, an extremely interesting and fine example of the rich gothic-Cordobese style. Further ahead is the EPISCOPAL PALACE, formerly the Caliphal Alcázar. Constructed in the XVth Century by Bishop Sancho de Rojas, it was destroyed by fire in 1745 and later rebuilt in its present form. The simplicity of its style is in perfect harmony with the rectangular form of the Mosque, and constitutes a remarkable architectural monument, being particularly notable in this richly decorative corner of the city. From here, the unrivalled southern aspect offers the eyes the softly undulating green countryside and the tall column of San Rafael cutting the horizon near the river; this is another monument by Vediguier, and fulfills its aesthetic function of completing an open space in the landscape without hiding anything.

To the left of the *Triunfo* is the *Puerta del Puente,* commissioned by Felipe II, and erected by Hernán Ruiz in 1571. Its golden mass, decorated with sculptures by Torrigiano, gives a grace and dignity to the bridge, which on its farther extremity is adorned by *La Calahorra,* an Arab type fortress, probably constructed in the XIVth Century. This houses the Historical Museum — MUSEO HISTÓRICO DE LA CIUDAD —, whose nine rooms and two towers contain important documents relating to the town as well as many interesting objects.

This BRIDGE, originally Roman, links Córdoba with the district of *Campo de la Verdad;* an image of San Rafael dominates it with all the grace of the youths so wonderfully described by Lorca in one of his gypsy romances. There is no other corner in Córdoba where you can experience all the mysterious beauty of twilight as you can here; in this spot the Cordobese sky, of a soft deep blue, reflects all its golden and purple crepuscular splendour in the river below. Then the bridge appears to be made of living gold. The river seems to be dotted with dark green islands, covered with verbena and rose-bay trees. From islet to islet little stone dams break the surface of the water, which foams over them in singing cascades. Here and there, you can still see the remains of old mills among the water and the dams. The walls of Córdoba stretch far away into the sunset among the mossy fruit trees of the *Huerta del Alcázar.* And over there, once past the new bridge, the Bishop's Garden blends the soft outlines of its trees and plants with the fading light of the dusk. It is from this bridge too, that one can enjoy the most wonderful panorama of the city; the *paseo de la Ribera,* the Mosque, the *Triunfo* and the Gates of Córdoba, just as they are depicted in the old XVIIIth Century engravings.

On returning along *calle Torrijos,* turn off by *calle M. Corella,* to come to the old *plaza de la Paciencia,* at the end of which is a fine ogival porch and the CASA DE EXPÓSITOS, then, already in *calle Manríquez,* stop for a moment to look at the patio of N° 3, where you will be pleasantly surprised by the rich showiness of the windows and wall, and the opulence of the many-lobed arches set on caliphal style columns. We continue along *calle Deanes* and *calle del Buen Pastor;* in the latter there is a beautiful patio, rather like that of *calle Manríquez,* yet different too, in spite of the similarity of style. You must stop at N° 2, to see this architectural gem; the iron grille, complicated in its design, is like a veil drawn across this patio, rich in tones of green and red, through whose archway, constructed in imitation of that of the Mihrab is yet another little patio with an arch built in fantastic perspective. These patios are, however, exceptional here. In general, the Cordobese style of patio does not go in for a great show of colour, rather is it remarkable for the simple whiteness of its limewash; nor are there usually architectural extravagances — the patio has more the appearance of a little garden. Much more likely are the flagged floors on which are little terraces of earth, where jasmine and night scented stock grow in profusion, while in the middle will be a fountain, or a slender palm tree, or even a well, set against a wall, its mouth set about with pots of geraniums and trailing ferns. The sun-washed HOUSE OF THE CEAS is to be found in *plaza de Ángel de Torres;* this edifice is perhaps better known as *casa del Indiano.* Its XVth Century façade is clearly mudéjar, although there are traces of ogival influence in the adornment of the little balconies. Going on along *calle de Valladares,* across *plaza de Pineda* and along *calle de Leopoldo de Austria,* we come out in front of the old minaret of the *capilla de las Esclavas.* From there we make our way along *calle Barroso* and over *plaza de Sevilla* to *plaza de José Antonio.*

II. THE JEWISH QUARTER

This trip to the Jewish quarter of old Córdoba can be made in conjunction with the visit to the Mosque if you wish, as the two lie so close to one another, but if you are not in a hurry, and prefer to take your time in viewing each thing you come to, then we recommend you to make the two trips separately.

We start off from the church of San Nicolás de la Villa, an edifice situated to the extreme south of the *avenida del Gran Capitán.* This XVth Century CHURCH OF SAN NICOLÁS proudly displays one of the most beautiful Cordobese towers; its finely traced octagonal minaret, surmounted by a simple bell tower, makes it stand out among the towers of Córdoba.

Going along *calle* and *plaza de San Felipe,* we can notice on our way the little garden of the *Escuela Normal de Maestros* before coming out into *plaza de Ramón y Cajal,* where is the MILITARY GOVERNOR'S PALACE, formerly the church of San Felipe Neri. The façade of this structure is Herrerian in style and dates from the XVIIth Century, while the letters *A* and *B* over the figures which adorn the main balconies are supposed to be the initials of the great sculptor, Alonso Berruguete, the younger, who lived in Córdoba at that time.

Facing the *Gobierno Militar* we have the CASA DE LOS HOCES, the old revenue building, and typical of a Cordobese aristocratic town house; its garden is also characteristic of the taste of the old ruling classes in this city. Continuing on our way, we come out into *plaza de la Trinidad*, where the parish church of San Juan can be seen, and going on from here by *calle Sánchez de Feria*, a street that is remarkable for the large number of fine patios to be admired the whole of its length, we arrive at the PUERTA DE ALMODÓVAR, known in the Xth Century as *Bab-Yend*, which means Jews' Gate. Now we are on the threshold of the JEWISH QUARTER. This is the district in which the Cordobese Jew lived for centuries, until the general expulsion ordered by the Catholic Sovereigns in the XVth Century. The Jews also helped to give splendour to the city in which they lived; among the most illustrious names in its history is to be found that of Maimónides, the author of a famous book, *Guía de Descarriados*. Going along *calle de los Judíos* we arrive at the very heart of the Jewish quarter; you should particularly notice how narrow this street is, with its clean-swept flagged surface and its little houses, the homes of humble folk but rich with flowers, ironwork grilles and patios. N° 18 is the HEBREW SYNAGOGUE, which we enter through the house door as it lacks an independent means of access. This temple was sumptuously decorated, as might be expected in a Jewish community as rich and influential as was that of Córdoba, but the endless mutilations it has suffered through the centuries have reduced it to the almost bare shell that it is today. The last important spoliation was carried out in the XVIIIth Century, when the superb panelling was stripped and replaced by canework. Today, the visitor can regard the delicate picture of its white-washed *plasterwork*, carried out in mudéjar style and adorned with inscriptions from the Psalms. The wall on the right is the most interesting, as it is here that the small Tabernacle, which contained the *toras*[1] of the Pentateuch is conserved. A little farther up from the Synagogue is the opening to the labyrinth and secret *calle de Averroes*, undoubtedly Arab in origin, narrow, lonely and winding, it speaks to us of other ages, taking us back to that "distant Córdoba" of the poets which lives in the streets of the city and the fantasy of the passer-by. At the end of *calle de*

---

[1] *Toras:* Books of the Jewishlaw.

18

Averroes a double archway gives on to a view of the CHAPEL OF SAN BARTOLOMÉ, originally an annexe to the *Palacio de Almanzor,* the residence of Caliph Hixen II's famous Prime Minister; today this edifice furnishes us with a fine example of the transition style between romanesque and ogival architecture. The interior is mudéjar; a magnificent socle of glazed tiles, and complicated patterns in plasterwork cover the walls, which are further enriched by inscriptions in Arabic. This place, perhaps the most secluded corner in all Córdoba, overwhelms the senses with its air of nostalgia, and holds us in its enveloping mantle of peacefulness, giving us the sensation that in this place Time has stayed still in long past ages. From here, an incredibly narrow alleyway brings us out in front of the *Hospital de Agudos,* built in 1703 by order of Cardinal Salazar.

We turn back along the same alley to take a look at *plaza de las Bulas,* a spot that is profoundly Cordobese in character and breathes the very essence of the soul of the city. Here we find the MUSEO MUNICIPAL TAURINO and the adjoining *Zoco,* or marketplace, both of which have beautiful Andalusian patios. The *Museo Taurino* contains many valuable objects connected with bullfighting going back to the earliest days. There are collections of bullfighters' clothes, swords, posters, sculptures, photographs, pictures of all kinds and various personal property belonging to famous bullfighters. Especially interesting are the rooms dedicated to Guerra "Guerrita" and "Lagartijo", the latter containing his entire study, a bronze effigy of him by Mateo Inurria and many other objects. The Manolete Room is also interesting: apart from the cast of a jacent statue of this great bullfighter, carved by Amadeo Ruiz Olmos, who also designed his tomb, there are bullfighting pictures by Vázquez Díaz, Echevarría, Murciano, etc. The rooms dedicated to "Lagartijo Chico" and "Machaquito", with oil paintings by Roberto Domingo and sculptures by Benlliure, are also worth a visit. Altogether, this Museum is quite unique in Spain for its annals of the history of bullfighting.

On the ground floor of the same building, there is also an exhibition of Leatherwork, displaying examples of this traditional Moorish work which has so long been carried out in Córdoba. Altar pieces, chairs, caskets, etc., may be seen here.

There is also a Hall containing examples of local silverwork which was famous in the city from the time of the Xth Century Caliphate.

Beside the *Museo Taurino* is the *Zoco,* or Market, where all kinds of traditional crafts, ranging from saddle-bags to filigrain silver, may be seen. On leaving *calle Tomás Conde,* we find in front of us the expanse of *Campo Santo de los Mártires,* with its shady old garden, surrounded by the walls of the Episcopal Palace, the historic CASA DE LAS PAVAS — so called on account of the peacocks decorating the fronting of the main door — and the remains of the ancient ROYAL ALCÁZAR, built by order of Alfonso XI in 1328. This edifice became a prison and then fell into ruins and finally was hidden under a series of other buildings. Recently, however, these obstacles have been cleared away, leaving the old structure clearly visible. Skilful restoration has turned it into one of the most attractive monuments of the town, whose gardens and patios offer a charming setting for the May *Festival de los Patios Cordobeses.*

Apart from the walls and ruined towers, the main interest in this place is centred in the Gardens, where one can still enjoy to the full the charm of pastoral surroundings of archeological interest, with the soft golden picture of the towers, and the greenery, reflected in the still waters of two old ponds. The Arab walls of Córdoba shut off the gardens at the back, where the gentle breeze from the Guadalquivir is wafted over the trees and plants.

Adjoining the Alcázar Gardens is the *Cuartel de Sementales,* or army studfarm, in whose stables can be seen magnificent specimens of the finest breeds of horses, the Spanish-Arab and Arab strains being really outstanding. The garden of the *Sementales* Barracks, with its avenue of rose trees and its broad promenade opening on to the river landscape, is a spot that is hardly known, and yet it is a place that is very beautiful. To the west of the Barracks is the popular district of San Basilio, otherwise called the district of Alcázar Viejo, with its beautiful patios which are gorgeously decorated during the May Festival.

Towards the river, following its course from the Roman bridge to the new one, there is the *Avenida del Corregidor,* flanked by the old Moorish walls and towers. This avenue links up with the splendid *Avenida del Conde de Vallellano,* where one gets a fine view of the western walls. Broad gardens spread out on either side of this avenue which ends in the *Paseo de la Victoria.*

III. THE LOWER DISTRICTS: SAN FRANCISCO AND SAN PEDRO

A note of quiet charm, a cordial welcome for the traveller, a limitless profusion of inns and public-houses — with cafés on the street under the shade of acacias and orange trees in summer and little rooms with tables, having under them salamanders burning almond shells, in winter — the throaty cadences of a guitar and the spontaneous and clapping of a dancer, a concentration on a game of dominoes or the sad strains of a Flamenco *copla* sung in undertones; such are the pictures these districts have to offer you, and with them agreeable company of a frank and hospitable people.

As on previous trips, we set out from *plaza de José Antonio,* and go along *calle Jesús María* as far as *calle Rey Heredia,* which turns to the left and follows its narrow way, as cool as a balcony, and a study of shade and the dazzling white of limewashed houses. In *calle Rey Heredia,* facing the convent of the Incarnation, N° 13 is one of the most notable mansions in Córdoba, and one of the most delicately beautiful, with its exquisite patio, its light marble columns supporting the fine arching at the end, where, past the lovely grille, another patio, of a gracious elegance, draws all one's attention. Continuing along *calle del Horno del Cristo,* a very short street, we come out at *plaza de Jerónimo Páez,* where the HOUSE OF JERÓNIMO PÁEZ, — the Provincial Archeological Museum, with its vigorous Italian style front, with traces of Bramant influence, and the shady public garden, planted with orange trees and cedars, give a note of distinction to the place.

The immense variety of artistic riches carefully conserved here makes a visit to this Museum, without any doubt one of the most interesting in Spain, one of the highlights of your trip. In this edifice are housed neolithic objects, fossilized Neanderthal remains, Bronze Age utensils, phalarics [1], small war sickles, spears, brooches —, sculptures of totem animals, lions, bulls, and ex-votos which were brought here from the Iberian sanctuaries of Collado in the gardens of Jaén; Roman articles — mosaics, fragments of huge statues, altars, memorial stones, coins, glassware, lamps, household gods, jewels and ceramics —; important Visigoth remains — burial urns, dishes, collections of 5000 coins and the famous Treasure of Torredonjimeno (Jaén), composed of votive crowns and visigothic crosses. Here too are old Arab and mudéjar [2] objects, which, together with those in the Museo de Medina Azahara represent all the artistic grandeur of the Caliphat Age, the highest level of culture in Europe during the Xth Century; among the treasures to be seen are remains of palaces, toilet bowls, fountains worked with figures of lions, white marble capitals, window lattices from the Mosque, ceramics bearing strange animal and floral designs and glazed in a manganese green and blue on a ground of white enclosed in white tin, valuable specimens of silverware, inscriptions, mazes, minting dies, curb stones of wells; and mudéjar doorways in plaster, capitals from Santa Clara, 35 decorated tiles and important Mozarab remains.

From here, *calle de Romero de Torres* leads us to the *Arco del Portillo*, a typically Arab construction which gives character to this popular corner of Córdoba. We retrace our steps a little, to carry on our way along *calle Cabezas*. Here we have the old HOUSE OF THE MARQUESES DEL CARPIO, with its bare XVth Century facings adorned with little balconies and windows, and a great doorway giving on to a patio which has recently been reconstructed in accordance with the best Cordobese architectural traditions. On the right of *calle Cabezas* is the opening of *callejita de los Arcos,* an ancient way dating from Moslem times, to which tradition ascribes the tragic episode, half history, half legend, of the Infantes de Lara, whose heads were left exposed on the arches of this street; at least, Moslem historians have left us this story. From this sad spot we go on to *calle de la Feria,* also called *calle de San Fernando,* and then along *calle Lucano* to *plaza del Potro,* where we have the PROVINCIAL MUSEUM OF FINE ARTS, and the JULIO ROMERO DE TORRES MUSEUM OF PAINTING.

Plaza del Potro, with that of *los Dolores,* is the most interesting square in Córdoba; like the Zocodover of Toledo it was one of the busiest public places in the XVIth Century. Muleteers, carters and peasants all used to gather here for the livestock markets; the beautiful XVIth Century fountain is still preserved, as is the ancient POSADA DEL POTRO, which must have been here in the time of Pedro I of Castile, with whose name a legend concerning it is linked. Once through the spacious and clean entrance we find ourselves in a rectangular patio around which runs a continuous balcony, with wooden balustrades. The stables are to the right of the patio, the doors to the left, those on the first floor giving access to the travellers' bedrooms. As this inn is still frequented by countryfolk it has managed to maintain its traditional atmosphere. At one side of the square we have a monument of San Rafael, while at the far end we can contemplate a view of the landscape, covered with growing corn; the green gardens along the banks of the river complete the picture of this wonderful place, described by Cervantes in *Don Quijote* as being one of the most typical public squares of his time. It is in such places as this that one can admire the great personality and individuality which have made of them something different, and given them a special character that they still keep, even after the passage of centuries; such squares and places are the living antithesis of the reigning monotony of character in modern cities that have no traditions behind them. These odd corners are the priceless heritage of the cities in which they belong, and which have known how to preserve them; it is thanks to these last vestiges of an older and perhaps more gracious way of life that a city keeps its own personality and zealously guards its ancestral prestige.

Adjoining the façade of the Museum of Fine Arts you will see the *portico* of the *Hospital de la Santa Caridad de Nuestro Señor Jesucristo,* a XVth Century construction. This is where the MUSEUM OF FINE ARTS is now lodged, the entrance to this institution having been restored in perfect harmony with the architectural details of the main structure, adding dignity and grace to the square.

Let us go into the Museum and pause for a moment by a *patio* of orange trees and myrtle, where there are also a fountain and fine sculptures of classical beauty. The Museum is divided into two sections. The Museum of Fine Arts itself is a rich storehouse of works by Cordobese and Andalusian painters, displaying canvases by such artists as Pedro de Córdoba, Bartolomé Bermejo, Luis Morales, Valdés Leal, Ribera, Murillo, Zurbarán, Antonio del Castillo, Goya and some great XIXth Century masters; the salon devoted to sculpture is also interesting, having works by Julio Antonio, Benlliure, Mateo Inurria, and Querol.

This Museum is completed by the part dedicated to the great Cordobese painter, Julio Romero de Torres, the best loved and appreciated artist produced by Córdoba; in his canvases one can sense a faithful, yet live interpretation of the very essence of the native songs, the music of the guitars, the landscape, the women, and the very soul of the Cordobese. His famous collection of paintings of women of this region is a very gallery of portraits which capture both the personality and the atmosphere of the city. In the backgrounds of all his works, and in the predellas [1] of the most outstanding of them, you will be able to recognise well known places in Córdoba, reproduced with great artistry by the master and filled with a poetry that is composed of a bitter melancholy, of utter nostalgia and of overpowering love for his native city. Popular sentiment pays unceasing homage to this great Cordobese painter :

...y aquel pintor con aire
    de gran torero...
	...that painter, with his air
	    of a great bullfighter...

In Julio Romero de Torres, Córdoba finds and loves its old traditions and that "Flamenco breeding", which, although it too is disappearing, is still to be discovered in pure blooded Cordobese.

Having left the Museum — and with the secluded *plaza de Aguayos* at our right, there is the church of San Pedro, the former Mozarabic cathedral —, we go along *calle de Armas,* where the popular atmosphere at once tells us, especially if we go there in the morning, that we are approaching all the colour and life of *plaza de la Corredera,* so called because in the XVIth and XVIIth Centuries it was here that were celebrated the bullfights, ribbon fights, cane fights, and other national sports and pastimes

At the present time one can see the whole *plaza* well, the covered market that used to stand in the centre now having been removed. This has been a great improvement, restoring all its old flavour of a XVIth Century square, a huge rectangle surrounded by porticoed galleries and triple metal balconies. This is the place in which the seamier side of Cordobese life used to gather during the golden years of the Spanish Empire. This great square still retains something of a raffish air and strongly conserves its popular character through its particular industries of esparto ware (baskets, panniers, hats and kitchen fans), old eating houses, popular inns, taverns and portable stalls.

---

[1] Lower part of a picture.

24

Going up *calle de la Espartería,* we come out facing the TOWN HALL, built where there was a Roman amphitheatre, according to a supposition made in the last century. The grand staircase of black marble is worth looking at, and hung above it is a fine painting representing San Rafael, by Antonio del Castillo.

The second street on the right of *calle Claudio Marcelo* takes us to the building of the CÍRCULO DE LA AMISTAD, where the patios, and the salons hung with paintings belonging to the first epoch of Romero de Torres are well worthy of a visit, as is the bullfighting hall, with its souvenirs of *Guerrita,* and the trophies won by the great bullfighter during his brilliant career.

Let us go along *calle Alfonso XIII,* as far as *plaza de Capuchinos,* otherwise called *plaza de Osio.* Osio, Bishop of Córdoba, presided over the Council of Nicea, where the Nicene Creed was put together, and through this, the name of Osio is known in all the Church. The monument which adorns the place has been dedicated to him by the city. At the far end is the front of the CAPUCHIN CONVENT, founded by the Duque de Sessa in 1655. The XVIIIth Century church has a fine painting by Palomino.

Calle M. Bañuelos brings us to the tiny *plaza de San Miguel,* where we have the XVIIth Century CHURCH of the same name. Its main façade is built in the transition style between romanesque and gothic, and is outstanding for its great limewashed rose window. The lateral door on the right is completely mudéjar. It will be seen that mudéjar influences are a constant factor in Cordobese architecture, and one quite often finds this style linked with other, different, and more classical styles. The interior is notable for the *capilla del Baptisterio,* where the primitive style and atmosphere are still preserved, displaying the fervour of mediaeval Christianity in the heart of the modern city. Here is a true echo of noble cavaliers, and all the splendour of the the the faith of the Holy King, Fernando III of Castille, the conqueror of the city.

IV. SANTA MARINA: THE BULLFIGHTERS' QUARTER

It is an inexplicable coincidence that the picturesque quarter of Santa Marina should be the birthplace of the great masters of the art of bullfighting. Here were born two of the most wonderful aces of the National Fiesta, two who have left their imperishable imprint on this ancient sport: *Lagartijo el Viejo,* and *Guerrita.* And following in the wake of such stars, a host of matadores, novilleros, banderilleros and picadores [1], who have all shone in the front ranks of the men who hazard their lives cheerfully: *Pepete, Bocanegra, Manene, El Torero, El Conejo, Rafaelito Molina, Manolete el Padre, Bebémayor, Bebéchico, Machaquito, Camará, El Zurito, Martorell, Lagartijo, Rafaelito Sánchez Saco...* Like don José Moreno *Onofre,* that great authority, we also are inclined to ask:

Córdoba, dime el misterio	Córdoba, explain this mystery
que no atino a comprender	That I have never understood,
el porqué nacieron todos	Why is it they are all
en el Campo la Merced...	Born in Campo de la Merced...

Leaving *plaza de José Antonio,* and going along *calle de Cruz Conde* and *avenida del Generalísimo,* we make our way to *Campo de la Merced.* The middle of the open space is covered by a thickly planted garden. On the left of the traveller arriving from *avenida del Generalísimo* is the old *convento de la Merced,* a churrigueresque pile built 1745, with a lovely entrance, flanked by Solomonic columns. The chapel of this convent, built in the same style,

---

[1] The *matador* is the chief torero of the *cuadrilla* (team), and his job is essentially to play the bull with the *muleta* (a bar of wood from which hangs the red cloth), and kill it. A *novillero* is a young *matador,* who begins his professional career by killing bulls of two to three years old, known as *novillos.* The *banderillero* is a torero attached to a matador's *cuadrilla,* his job being to plant the *banderillas* in the bull (the *banderillas* are thin sticks of wood, with an iron barb on one end, the shaft being decorated with coloured paper; they must be planted in the thick nape of the bull's neck). The *picador* is the mounted torero who must catch the bull's rush with a a sort of pike.

and today used as the PROVINCIAL HOSPICE, has an interesting retable on the High Altar, and a statue of Christ Crucified which originally came from Antequera, being brought to Córdoba in the XIVth Century; tradition has it that Christopher Columbus prayed in front of this statue during his stay in the Mercedarian House. The main patio, a fine example of baroque architecture, follows clean and balanced lines, with its columns and pavements of white marble and its great staircase of coloured marble. We cross the gardens to the north-east of *Campo de la Merced*. In this corner we have the legendary TORRE DE LA MALMUERTA, which Enrique III of Castile ordered to be built in 1405. Octagonal in shape, and surmounted by sharply outlined battlements, it used to be linked with the city wall, in which an arch was constructed; today it appears isolated from the rest of old Córdoba, and surrounded by modern buildings. The interior is especially remarkable for its spacious, hall, with a vaulted roof that is a marvel of stone filigree, and a staircase leading to the upper terrace, from which we can enjoy a very interesting panoramic view. The name of *Malmuerta* (bad death) takes its origin from the legend of a knight wo was unjustly jealous of his wife, an innocent woman, and killed her; as a punishment the King obliged him to pay for the cost of raising this tower. This old story, handed down to us by Vaca de Alfaro, has served to create an atmosphere of mystery around the old tower and has had rather a powerful effect on the popular imagination in the course of past centuries.

The *Torre de la Malmuerta* will soon be dedicated to the exaltation of the sons of Córdoba who took part in the colonialisation of America in the XVth, XVIth and XVIIth Centuries.

Having *avenida Obispo Pérez Muñoz* ahead, we see on our left the CONVENT DE CARMELITAS DESCALZOS OF SAN JOSÉ DE CÓRDOBA, more commonly known as SAN CAYETANO. Situated on a low hill, on the slopes of which a little garden has recently been planted, the XVIIth Century Graeco-Romano pile of the church rears its noble mass of dark stone above the white walls enclosing the outer patio of the convent. Sombre green cypresses peep out over the top of this wall, and an air of spiritual withdrawal from the outer world impresses itself on the visitor. The pleasant landscapes of the Sierra de Córdoba form a harmonious background to this Carmelite convent as they softly fade into the far horizon.

As we pass through the *Puerta del Colodro* we enter the very heart of Santa Marina. On the right, in *plaza de Lagunilla,* we observe a simple and moving monument to the ever mourned *Manolete,* the greatest Spanish bullfighter of all time. *Manolete* was not born in this quarter, but in that of San Miguel, in *calle Torres Cabrera*; he grew up however, and learned the fundamentals of his art in Santa Marina, which is proud to claim him as one of its sons. We follow calle Mayor de SANTA MARINA as far as the parish church of the quarter, bearing the same name, the most beautiful church in all Córdoba. There is quite an air of a mediaeval fortress about this pile, which seems to breathe of deeds of chivalry. Its entrances are romanesque, and the windows gothic, while the great bell tower was built in the XVIIth Century; the church has three naves, terminating in polygon shaped apses, and its fine vaulted roof is covered with magnificent panelling. Apart from the main retable, we would also draw to your attention the statue of the *Virgen de la Guía,* a masterpiece by Gómez de Sandoval, the retable of the altar dedicated to the *Virgen del Rosario,* with paintings by Antonio del Castillo, and the entrance to the Orozco Chapel, showing a XVth Century mudéjar influence.

Toreros, piconeros [1] and singers, these are the human flowers of this quarter:

Por Santa Marina entré	I was going into Santa Marina
salieron los piconeros	When the *piconeros* were leaving
que me querían comé...	Who wanted to eat me...

Here are to be seen stone paved streets, with green mosses growing between the cracks, little cut-off squares, the old cypresses of the CONVENT DE SANTA ISABEL, and streets with names like *Moriscos, Tafures, Marroquíes,* and *Yedra,* where one breathes yet more intensely the atmosphere of old traditions, and older customs. *Calle de Santa Isabel* leads us right to the door of the convent of the same name, where the secluded patio, with the soft shade of its cypresses, welcomes us like a haven of sunshine, limewashed walls and sweet smells, inviting us to pause for a moment's reflection and feel the tide of peacefulness sweep over our inner selves, away from the noise and worries of the outer world.

The famous CASA DE DON GOME proudly displays its michelangelesque entrance on this street, with shields and arms of the

---

[1] A *piconero* is a man who either manufactures or sells a type of charcoal known as *picón,* which is especially suitable for salamanders.

Saavedra family, and Collars of Carlos III and the Toisón de Oro (the Golden Fleece). Once through the porch, we find ourselves in a Tuscan-Andalusian style patio, with a tall palm tree in the middle and climbing plants trailing over the walls. The magnificent staircase, covered with rich octagonal working, reflects mudéjar taste. But what always most attracted the curiosity of the tourist and stirred the imagination of the Cordobese were the fourteen patios of this fine house. Secret and beautiful patios where an eternal Spring unfolds all the riotous glory of its colours, where roses and jasmine twine themselves round the trunks of the fig trees, where carnations and geraniums alternate with myrtle and box-wood trees, where the sweet-basil blends its perfume with the spicy aromas of orange and lemon trees, and dahlias and hollyhocks flaunt their brightness against the old grilles in front of the windows. Enchanted corners, embellished with fountains, wells, and delicate statuary gracefully posed here and there, while overhead is the unceasing song and chatter of the birds as they flit from branch to branch, and the soft lullaby of countless white doves. (This was formerly the residence of the Villaseca family, and now belongs to the Marqués de Viana.)

Continuing on our way, let us follow *calle Juan Rufo* to the *Fuenseca*. This lovely corner of Córdoba is enlivened by the fountain of *Fuenseca;* it was originally built in 1760, but alterations carried out in 1808 left it in its present form. We go from here into *calle de Alfaros,* and going up the gradient of *Cuesta del Bailío* we reach plaza de Capuchinos, otherwise known as *plaza de los Dolores.*

Cuesta del Bailío... How the very soul of Córdoba sings to us in this spot, as intimate as a garden plot:

de rodillas la he subío.	Even the cuesta del Bailío,
por tu querer, mi serrana,	For your love, my soul's fate,
Hasta la cuesta el Bailío	Have i climbed on my knees.

Plaza de Capuchinos, lovely by day, is an enchantment at night, above all if the moon is shining. Harmonious of line, white and simple, with the greatly venerated *Cristo de los Dolores* facing the façade of the Capuchin convent on the far side of the plaza, and the *Hospital de San Jacinto,* another noble building of simple lines, the whole place inspires in us such a feeling of inner peace and tranquility as might be said to be created by its limpid, fervent air, and reinforced by countless devotions. An emotion like that inspired by a *saeta*[1] stirs our soul. This is brought about by an indefinable something that brings the celestial coolness of true religious feeling to calm the tragic heat of human passions.

Pause awhile in this place at night to listen to Córdoba's heart beating among the stars. Stay for a moment at the feet of the *Cristo de los Dolores,* and from there gaze on the whole of the place, with its familiar outlines. Then raise your eyes to Christ's face and see how His crucified body is cast in a play of light and shadow from the lamps. And don't go away without seeing the VIRGEN DE LOS DOLORES *in* her shrine in *San Jacinto.* She is the most loved statue of the Cordobese, who publicly show their fervour and devotion to this Image on the afternoon of Good Friday.

V. FROM SAN PABLO TO PUERTA NUEVA

Every district has its own personality. The trip we call *San Pablo - Puerta Nueva* covers the south-eastern part of the city, cutting across a busy popular quarter, noisy and happy, centred on the parish church of San Lorenzo. We begin our walk in *plaza del Salvador,* adjoining the Town Hall, where we can see the Solomonic entrance to the CONVENTO DE SAN PABLO, added to the main body of the convent in 1706; the convent itself is a romanesque-gothic-mudéjar structure which San Fernando ordered to be built in 1241. Going down a little staircase, we find ourselves in a little, damp, green patio, at the end of which is the entrance to the church, reconstructed in the XVIIIth Century in place of the primitive XVth Century edifice. The interior comprises three naves covered by a finely worked ceiling, which is supported by wide arches on massive pillars; here it is spacious, beautiful of line, and full of grace and strength, and this interior undoubtedly represents the purest Cordobese gothic. We leave by the door on the left, restored by Mateo Inurria, the only one of the original doors that is still preserved; it is splay-arched on Moslem capitals.

Calle de San Pablo, calle de Santa Marta; here, on the left, we have the CONVENTO DE SANTA MARTA, an establishment belong-

---

[1] Couplets which are sung spontaneously during the passage of a procession in Holy Week.

ing to the nuns of the Order of San Jerónimo. A patio full of rustic charm gives access to the chapel. The whiteness of the limewash, the greenery of the jasmine, and the night scented stock combine to give this place its own special atmosphere of peace — a peace that is not of this world, and that is sensed in every corner of the patio.

The entrance to the chapel is gothic in style and richly ornamented. The interior is composed of one ogival nave and apse.

Returning to *calle de San Pablo,* we continue down this street as far as *plaza de Orive,* which is on the right, dominated by the sumptuous plateresque MANSION OF THE VILLALÓN FAMILY — a place rich in legends and stories of apparitions and mysterious disappearances.

We go back again to *calle de San Pablo,* and follow it until we come to *plaza de San Andrés,* where is the HOUSE OF COMENDADOR LUNA, remarkable for its fine corner balcony divided by a slender column, and its old patio and superb staircase.

The parish church of San Andrés rears itself, yellow and white, in the open place of which it is the main feature. As we make our way along this crowded street, animated with the comings and goings of all manner of people, we come to the *Realejo,* one of the main street crossings of this quarter. We continue by *calle Santa María de Gracia,* stopping now and then at any one of the numerous taverns; at the end of the street can be seen the beautiful entrance and tower of SAN LORENZO, another parish church, which dominates the plaza of the same name. Its porticoed atrium, the splendour of its rose window, its romanesque fortress abutting on its gothic gracefulness and mudéjar decorative detail, its finely proportioned tower, like an imprint on the blue skies, and the harmonious lines of the whole architectural entity make of this church of San Lorenzo one of the loveliest structures in the city. As in many another popular place, an agreeable vitality and liveliness reigns here, holding sway until the small hours of the morning. Countless stalls, wine shops, public-houses with flowered patios and terraces, all combine to give it the air of an old market place. Here can be sensed the memory of other days. The people live, do business, stroll and amuse themselves in these streets; in this quarter life passes out of doors, in the open place and in the public house.

But nearby lies dreaming that "Córdoba, distant and remote" discovered by Lorca. It is quite sufficient to follow the *Arroyo de*

31

San Rafael, which takes us to *plaza San Rafael,* in whose CHURCH the image of the Guardian Archangel of the city is venerated; or we can continue our stroll along *Arroyo de San Lorenzo* and *calle del Crucifijo,* to come out in *plaza de la Magdalena,* where there is a HERMITAGE of the same name. An old garden of gnarled trees, little white and yellow houses that might belong to any southern village, and the old gold of the church, softened by the moss which sprouts where there is neglect, and the beauty of decay, together strike a note of romanticism. Going back to *Arroyo de San Lorenzo,* and continuing along it as far as the *Puerta Nueva,* another important centre of Cordobese life, we find there the stopping place for the buses which will take us back to the heart of the city.

VI. THE SIERRA DE CÓRDOBA

Córdoba is delightfully situated between two complementary geographical-economic regions, such as are the *Campiña* and the *Sierra,* reaping great benefits from its situation, and many pretty little chalets and cottages can be seen dotted about the slopes of the Sierra. In its constant desire to attain the heights and smell the fragrance of the pine forests, the city spreads itself as far as the *Huerta de los Arcos* and along the *carretera del Brillante.* The landscape of hills and wooded mountain slopes, the lower terraces shaded by great fruit orchards, evergreen oaks, carob trees, cork oaks, pines, almond trees and palm trees, the agaves and prickly pear trees seen by the roadside or sprawling their savage greenery over an outcrop of rock — all this sharply calls to mind an African scene. And the scrub covering the continuous wall of mountains along the northern horizon gives the Sierra that characteristic bluish grey colour through which it has come to be known as the *Sierra Morena:*

¡Qué bien los nombres ponía	How well they chose the name,
quien puso Sierra Morena	Whoever gave Sierra Morena
a esta Serranía!	To this long range!

The Sierra is inseparably linked with the city. During the Roman epoch of Celtiberian rebellions, the guerrillas and Virithus' hosts swept as far as the walls of Córdoba, a Roman municipality, which they had to attack from the mountains. In the time of the Moslem domination, countless monasteries flourished, teaching philosophy and ascetism amid the crags of the Sierra, whither the Mozarabs took refuge, fleeing from the rich and exquisite Court life in the capital of the Caliphate. Such monasteries were those of *Santa María de Cuteclara,* and *Peñamellaria,* whose ruins can still be seen among the red oleanders and fragrant rock roses. Later still, in the XIXth Century, the Sierra became the bulwark of guerrillas and patriots against the Napoleonic invasion, and, of _ourse, the legendary domain of the bandits who have left such picturesque images engraved on the popular imagination.

This song *por serranas* still recalls that romantic era:

Va una partía	A group is going
por la Sierra Morena,	Through the Sierra Morena,
va una partía,	A group is going
va una partía,	A group is going
y al capitán le llaman	And its captain is called
José María.	José María.
No será preso	They'll never catch him
mientras su jaca torda	While his dapple grey cob
tenga pescuezo...	Can still run...

The preference for a *quinta,* or mountain chalet, is Latin and Arab in its origin, and Córdoba, Roman and Moorish in its history, still retains this taste for country life. It is for this reason that a mountain itinerary could not possibly be omitted as a complement to the trips made in the city itself.

Four country excursions are sufficient to see, and to know, the most notable of the Sierra: MEDINA AZAHARA, MONASTERIO DE SANTO DOMINGO, LA ARRUZAFA, and LAS ERMITAS.

MEDINA AZAHARA. Medina Azahara is situated 8 kilometres out of Córdoba, in the western part of the Sierra, a site chosen for the vast fortress on account of its mild winters, protected from cold winds. The Almodóvar road brings us on the way to Medina Azahara, which is on the right. Before arriving at the Cordobese Versailles, we pass, 6 kilometres from the city, the ruins of Alamiriya, built by Almanzor, the powerful Prime Minister of Hixen II. The Alamiriya was a sort of Medina Azahara in miniature, modelled on the Alcázar of Abderrahman III.

Medina Azahara, surrounded by olive trees and plantations of evergreen oaks, and shaded by mountain pines, is today simply a vast site of ruins. Among the many legends about its origin, perhaps the most popular is that which affirms it was constructed in honour of Zahara ("The Flower"), favourite wife of Caliph Abderrahman III.

Against this charming supposition however, we must consider reasons of a political-military nature which must have heavily influenced the monarch in his important decision to abandon Córdoba, capital of his dynasty, and transfer the whole centre of political life to a new city, built by himself. Medina Azahara was therefore, palace, court and city. It had a population of more than 12.000, and all the important sections of the State administration were quartered there. Such a place calls to mind similar royal residences: the Fortress of the Great Victories of Pharaoh Rameses II, and the Palace-Court of Versailles.

The first foundations were sunk in 936, under the supervision of three famous architects: Abdallah ben Yunus, Hasan ben Mohammed, and Ali ben Chafar, an Egyptian. If we are to believe the Moslem historians, especially Almakari and El Edrisi, 10.000 men worked for over 25 years preparing and carrying the materials which went into its construction.

The city covered a vast area, on three natural terraces. According to El Edrisi the palaces and pavilions of the Caliph were on the upper terrace. Among splendour so great that it stupefied the ambassadors of the contemporary court of Constantinople, and the Kings of León who visited Medina in person, Sancho I and Ordoño IV, the most outstanding feature was the hall known as the Salon of the Caliphs, with its ceiling of gold mosaics its delicate windows of transparent marble, the central pond made of porphyry and filled with mercury, and the wonderful pearl, a gift of the Emperor of Constantinople, which hung in dazzling light from the finely worked ceiling. As in the Mosque, horseshoe arches and multilobed arches were predominant, with marble columns many of them of Roman style, and Corinthian capitals of the kind known as "beehive capitals", from the way in which their elaborate design recalls the honeycombs of a beehive. In general, the most interesting feature of the city was its richly decorative aspect, this being the most original facet of the art of the era. Byzantine influence, strongly visible in the adornment of the Mosque, is here diminished, and African and Oriental currents can be noticed. The decorations were not worked directly on the buildings, but were done apart and then appliqued to the structure, which was magnificently covered, one might even say tapestried, with thin sheets of stucco and plasterwork in which the arabesque was the leading motif, that is, geometric and orthodox designs were followed, though plant and flower shapes were also used, as were inscriptions of verses from the Koran.

On the upper terrace is the extraordinarily rich MUSEUM OF MEDINA AZAHARA, where is kept a wonderful artistic treasure, the result of the excavations. At the present time, those responsible are working on a partial archeological reconstruction of the palace. One example of this reconstruction can be seen in the *salón de Abderramán III,* the most magnificent and interesting apartment, built between 954 and 957, under the direction of Shunaif.

Unfortunately, the life of Medina Azahara was ephemeral. The political-military chaos ensuing after the death of Almanzor in 1002 let loose a rabble of Berber mercenary troops, who sacked Medina Azahara with great barbarism in 1010. Succeeding waves of African invaders, drawn by the fame and sumptuousness of the marvellous palace, again looted the city a number of times. Already, by the time of Felipe II, this fantastic place was a heap of ruins. Time, like the mythological sea that swallowed Vineta and Atlantis, destroyed the dream mansion of the Andalusian Caliphs while it was yet at the height of its opulence.

Now that you have a brief idea of the pathetic history of this great monument, let us take a look at the remains that offer themselves for your admiration in blocks of vain and fantastic reconstruction. Medina Azahara invites you to contemplate her finely worked stones, her delicate glass, her urns and her lovely ceramics; she is proud to show you her fragments of rich ornamentation and her coins of gold and silver. She offers you a journey through time, the shade of her lovely trees and the canopy of the sky above her; names, lands, sounds from the past and sentiment that will pluck your heartstrings, power that has fallen into dust and desires that have drifted away on the wind like a summer cloud — all these have been hers and all these she displays if you have a perceptive mind and can appreciate spiritual things.

35

Look at this wonderful land, that one might say had been gilded by the reflections from old wines and older gold; observe the mellow sunlight, flowing over the stones like clear honey, and see how the poppy pushes its upward way through what remains of forgotten halls and salons. And if you should be caught here by the dusk, wait a while and notice how the moonlight, one jewel that has escaped the ravages of time, restores new richness to this fantastic dream city of the Cordobese monarchy.

Near Medina Azahara is the noble pile of the MONASTERIO DE SAN JERÓNIMO DE VALPARAÍSO, founded by Fray Vasco de Souza, a monk of the Order of St. Jerome, in the XVth Century, and magnificently endowed by doña Inés de Pontevedra, widow of don Martín Fernández de Córdoba, the Alcaide de los Donceles.

This superb monastery remained in the hands of the Hieronymite Order until the XIXth Century, when the brethren were expelled. At the present time it is the property of the Marqués del Mérito, and it is to the Mérito family that we owe its present fine state of preservation.

The entrance is solemn in its simplicity, and the gothic cloister is at once gracious and severe in line. Materials brought from the ruins of Medina Azahara must have been used in the construction of this great foundation. Especially interesting are the "*In pace*", the refectory, the Chapter Hall, and what are known as the King's rooms, where Isabel *la Católica,* Felipe II, and Felipe VI were all lodged during their sojourns in this monastery.

MONASTERIO DE SANTO DOMINGO. The Monastery of Santo Domingo is situated in the very heart of the Sierra de Córdoba, buried in a fragrant valley among streams and pine forests. In the sanctuary of this sacred spot the XVth Century figure of the *Santísimo Cristo de San Álvaro* is venerated. The community was founded by San Alvaro, a Dominican monk, and from its earliest days the fame of the miracles wrought through the intercessions of the brethren spread over all the Sierra. A number of hermitages were constructed, in which San Alvaro and the other brethren dedicated themselves to the difficult exercises of asceticism, hidden away from the outer world. And today, all that remains of these lonely retreats is an occasional ruined wall on the crest of a hill.

The Sanctuary however is quite well preserved, although it has been frequently enough touched up during the past five centuries. It has a fine retable, and the walls are decorated with ingenious symbolical paintings. Above all, the figure of Christ Crucified, which tradition says appeared miraculously to San Alvaro, is still preserved here.

Not only the Sanctuary is worth seeing, but also the path, from which a visitor can enjoy interesting views. Once past the estates known as *Maestre de Escuela, La Viñuela,* and *El Jardinito,* we have on the left of the way a stone cross which commemorates a miracle of San Alvaro, while on the right is the rushing *Arroyo de los Cedros.* As we gradually approach the Sanctuary, so our surroundings call more strongly to mind the Holy Places. It was for this reason that the founder of the monastery chose the site as a place of retreat from the world and penitence for past sins. Fray Luis de Granada, the famous preacher and a master of Spanish prose, as well as a Brother of the Order of San Alvaro, lived here for a time; it was in these surroundings that he wrote his moving *Guía de Pecadores* in the XVIth Century, a volume that is as renowned throughout Christendom as the *Imitation of Christ* or the *Introduction to the Devotional Life,* of St. Francis de Sales.

The Santo Domingo road links with that of *El Brillante* at a spot called the *Puentecillo,* a kilometre out of Córdoba.

LA ARRUZAFA. *La Arruzafa* is yet another interesting place out of the city, being a mountain *parador* built on the ruins of a palace for recreation, of Abderrahman I, which later became a residence of the Franciscan Order.

It is situated on a rise, to the left of the old road to the Hermitages, in front of a spot known as *Cañito Basán,* about two kilometres from Córdoba.

On account of its magnificent gardens of palm trees, and orange groves, its little refreshment establishments and the terraces from which one can enjoy superb views of Córdoba, this charming place has become one of the favourite and most appreciated sites in the whole Sierra. The old palace has now been converted into a splendid "Parador de Turismo" where travellers may stay and enjoy all the delights of the mountains of Córdoba.

LAS ERMITAS. The *Ermitas* which can be seen from Córdoba, crowning the mountains tops of the Sierra, call to mind the old refuges and monastic communities of the Mozarabs during the epoch of the Caliphate. The road to *El Brillante* links with that to *Las Ermitas* at milestone 11, corresponding in height to that of the *Lagar de la Cruz*. This *El Brillante* road runs through thick rows of acacias and brambles, while on either side rise the terraces, domes and turrets of countless little chalets across small orchards or gardens, which are always a blaze of colour, whatever the season. On reaching the *Venta del Brillante,* to the left begins the stretch of the road leading to *Las Ermitas* — this way is hardly to be recommended for cars. We prefer to continue along the *El Brillante* road as far as the ranch known as *Granito de Oro,* and from there go to *Huerta de los Arcos,* superbly situated on the very skirts of the Sierra, and dominating a vast panorama of the city and the surrounding countryside. A track leads up to the gates of this estate, which is included in all itineraries, as much for the elegant lines of its Arabs architecture as for the charm of its promenades and its gardens embellished with old stone benches and fine specimens of statuary. Cypresses, orange trees and palms alternate with magnolias, rose trees and box-wood, while ornamental pools and fountains give added grace and beauty to shady corners, lawns and terraces.

Just about one kilometre further ahead we come to the *Cerrillo,* and there take the road to the left, following it as far as *Las Ermitas,* some 15 kilometres from Córdoba.

A great monumental image of the Sacred Heart of Jesus dominates the hill, enclosed by a rough wall of stones and earth, where we find the hermitages. We ring the little bell, and, after quite an interval, which at least gives us time to observe the vastness of the plain, the porter finally opens the door and invites us to enter. Ahead of us stretches a long avenue of cypresses, severe and beautiful, bordering on a shady orange grove, at the far end of which little rustic pools gleam like mirrors; this avenue leads us to a chapel where the hermits celebrate their offices.

The Hermitages are scattered about at quite a distance from one another, as, although the hermits come under monastic rules they still maintain old traditions of isolation and retreat. Their code of regulations was established by Fray Diego Mardones, Bishop of Córdoba, in the XIVth Century. Amongst the most illustrious of the hermits, we might mention the Marqués de Villaverde, who, in the XVIIIth Century, forsook the world and took up his abode in these solitary places for the rest of his life. The hermits divide their time between prayer, work, and the practice of charity; they live on alms and the products of their own work, and at midday they distribute soup to the poor of the surrounding villages.

From the foot of the monument of the Sacred Heart of Jesus we can look out over a remarkable landscape; from here can be seen the *Sierras de Cabra* and *de Priego,* and on very fine days the far-away Grenadine peaks of the *Sierra Nevada;* the meandering green mirror of the Guadalquivir, and the lovely countryside, emerald coloured in winter and spring, and richly golden in summer and autumn; and like stains on a tapestry, the dazzling whiteness of distant villages, Espejo, Castro del Río, Bujalance...

CORDOBESE FOLKLORE

If there is one region of Spain where the various popular manifestations of traditional folklore are a reality that is inseparable from the history of the province, from its religion, and from its very nature, that region is Andalusia. The Andalusian, delicately equating the Spaniard, goes around the world singing and talking about Spain with an eloquence and graciousness that are unrivalled by any other Spanish region, not even by Castile itself. Andalusian folklore has spread out and over local and regional limits to assume a national Spanish quality and a transcendence in universal art: Holy Weeks, bullfights, popular pilgrimages, country fiestas, Flamenco singing, dances, fairs and outdoor entertainments. Where can you find the equal to such rich traditions? Andalusian folklore has its place as much in a dramatic work by Lorca as in a poem by Alberti [1] or a musical composition by de Falla [2] because this particular folklore is possessed of two great qualities which can so rarely be found together — artistry and popular taste... The wail of a *saeta* rising from the singer's throat like the song of a wild bird, soars through a heaven of ancient musical lore yet never breaks out of a certain unwritten limit, within which, however, it has a mysterious freedom of expression. The fervour of Holy Week

[1] Rafael Alberti, a great contemporary Andalusian poet. [2] Manuel de Falla, the most important Spanish composer of his epoch (1876-1951).

surges from a consciousness that is overflowing with religious feeling, but this spontaneous fervour is multiplied by the sheer beauty of the processional *pasos*[1] and stimulated by the breathtaking luxury of such solemn events.

And what more delicate could you find than an Andalusian singer? He is always a soloist who will have nothing to do with choirs. Here Spanish individualism at its best gives a vibrant something to the lone voice. Imagine the scene: everybody is silent, one might almost say there is a religious hush cast over them; the first chords plucked from the guitar shiver in the air, then the skilful fingers of the *tocador*[2] induce melodies to flow from the strings, almost fugues as he improvises, yet the guitarist is always "in tone" with the singer and adjusts his spirit to the particular "mood" of the song. The guitar is much more than a mere cold accompaniment; it is a musical seduction which conjures the voice with ancient magic. Andalusian singing has so many subtle shades of tone that only very experienced ears can note the differences between the variations, and clearly distinguish a *fandango de Cabra*[3] from a *verdial,* for example. Liberty, which is the very essence of such music, permits within each style the coexistence of diverse personal variations; for instance, in the domain of *malagueñas* we have the *malagueña de Juan Breva*[4] side by side with that of *Chacón*[5].

One particular sort of singing will take any number of richly individual forms: the fandango has innumerable modalities. Without even leaving Córdoba we can hear the *fandango de Cabra* and that of Lucena, while in its turn the Cabra fandango again divides into the *fandango de Cayetano*[6] *(Niño de Cabra)* and the *fandango de Rivas*[7], the nearest approach to the verdials and the *malagueñas*. The same thing occurs with the dances.

Elsewhere we qualified Córdoba as the capital of singing, and it is a fact that serious songs have their centre here. The *soleá,* which changes so much according to the district, is plainly Cordo-

---

[1] An effigy sculptured group representing one of the scenes of Christ's Passion, and carried in procession in Holy Week. [2] The guitarist who accompanies the *cantor* or vocalist. [3] Variations of *cante hondo* and *cante flamenco.* [4] Juan Breva, a Malagueño and an important figure in *cante hondo.* [5] Antonio Chacón, a Jerezano and the most important interpreter of *cante hondo.* [6] Cayetano, *Niño de Cabra,* a *cantaor* who followed Chacón's school of singing with great success. [7] Rafael Rivas, an outstanding interpreter of the *fandango de Córdoba.*

bese, and here in Córdoba it acquires the pithy tone which she distinguishes it from other songs:

No preguntes por saber,	Don't ask just to know
que el tiempo te lo dirá,	What Time will later tell you,
que no hay cosa más bonita	There is nothing more beautiful
que saber sin preguntar...	Than to know without asking...

The *alegría de Córdoba,* which is thought by some to have originated with the Cadiz Marismas, is a song which, whether it was born here or not, has become naturalised in this city, where it has been handed down from one generation to the next for over a century and a half.

The *serranas,* long songs heard in the mountains, taking their inspiration from pastoral themes, love, and the banditry of the last century, are also Cordobese from beginning to end. Besides these representative songs, in Córdoba they sing: *fandangos de Cabra* and of *Lucena, medias granadinas, seguidillas, fandangos de Huelva* and *Alosno, malagueñas, verdiales, tarantas mineras, cartageneras, alegrías de Cádiz, peteneras, farrucas, bulerías, tanguillos, polos, milongas*[1], etc.

Autonomous Flamenco dancing is typified by the *vito and the soleá*[2], and song and dance combined under the magic influence of a guitar are an unforgettable experience.

Singing is spontaneous in Córdoba, and this is why it is always so authentic. There really are no determined places in which you can hear it, and it is not something that is exploited to attract tourists. A song will be offered you as a mark of friendship, and to honour a stranger it will be given him with all the aristocratic grace that is so natural to the Cordobese; it is one of the most personal and intimate things there is about Córdoba.

These Flamenco songs are one of the highlights of all typical Cordobese fiestas; Fairs, Holy Week, Pilgrimages. Their most intimate surrounding is the tavern and the *perol.* But let us talk a little about the fiestas.

Holy Week, in perfect keeping with the serious and rather withdrawn character of the city, is the most austere of all Andalusia, beginning on Palm Sunday and ending on Easter Sunday

---

[1] Variations of *cante hondo* and *cante flamenco.* [2] Andalusian dances.

morning; in between, therefore, exists a week of religious processions, with luxuriously adorned *pasos* and superb sculptures, such as Our Lord Redeemed, by Francisco Pacheco (Palm Sunday), The Most Holy Christ Saviour of Souls (Maundy Thursday), The Most Holy Christ of Mercy (Wednesday of Holy Week), Our Lady of Sorrows, of which the Christ is by Juan de Mena (Maundy Thursday), and Our Lady of Sufferings (Good Friday).

Cordobese religious feeling reaches its full height on the Feast of San Rafael Archangel (24th of October), a day when everybody goes out to the country to have a jolly good *perol,* or lunch in the open air, the meal generally comprising a dish of rice and a wonderful variety of hors-d'œuvres, or *tapas,* which are dipped in wine, and keep the merrymakers going until lunch is ready, which usually is not until five or six o'clock in the afternoon; the day of *Nuestra Señora de la Fuensanta* (8th of October) is marked by a popular outdoor rejoicing in the *Campo Madre de Dios;* the Feast of the Assumption (15th of August) is a great holiday in the Mosque Quarter. The *Romería of the Santísimo Cristo de San Alvaro* is an occasion of great fervour, when the whole city makes a pilgrimage to the mountain sanctuary of Santo Domingo de Scala Cœli, and the valleys are filled with people (this Feast is celebrated on the fourth Sunday in Lent). Other typical religious events are the *Romería of Nuestra Señora de Linares,* another mountain trip, this time to the *Santuario de Linares;* Christmas Eve, New Year's Eve, the Feast of the Three Kings, Corpus Christi...

A particularly interesting festival is that of the Cordoban Patios, which is celebrated in the first fortnight of May, after the Seville fair. This is the time to visit the patios brimming over with flowers and the squares adorned with the popular and artistic May crosses, and see the town in its loveliest season.

Concerts of classical music, ballet, recitals of *cante hondo,* Spanish classical theatre, modern plays, operetta, Andalusian dancing, open air flamenco contests, in the Alcázar gardens, the patio of the Archaeological Museum, Jerónimo Páez Palace, etc., make the *Festival de los Patios Cordobeses* a unique occasion on which to get into the spirit of Andalusia and where you can see the flamenco art in its purest and most unadulterated form.

Among all these fiestas of more or less deep religious significance there is one great popular fiesta, that of the *Feria de Nues-*

tra Señora de la Salud (from 25th of May to 1st of June), when there are livestock fairs, bullfights, novilladas [1], concerts, dances, etc...

The September Fair (25th to 30th) is more intimate and localised, and marks the beginning of the Cordobese autumn, with its fiestas and dances. In both you will see all the products of local craftsmanship displayed for sale in numerous stalls and in all the shops; then you will see the things for which Córdoba has long been famous — embossed leathers, precious metalwork, ceramics, etc...

And if you want the soul of Córdoba to enter yet more deeply into your whole being, during these days you are among us, drink nothing but the fine *oloroso* wines of Montilla and Moriles, and in the restaurants you frequent, ask for typical Cordobese dishes: hare with *salmorejo* [2], frogs with tomatoes, stewed lamb, omelet paysanne, eggs *a como salgan,* eggs *a la flamenca,* oxtail stew, these latter being piquant dishes made from a basis of spices and vegetables; mushrooms, carrots, artichokes — a legacy from the oriental cuisine. Cordobese sweets and pastries still have their own specialities, like *pastel cordobés,* of puff paste and cider; the *perruna,* a sort of tart; *polvorones,* made from butter, flour and eggs; delicate sweets, like egg yolks and coconut, sweet peppers, pine nuts, and almonds...

This is Córdoba, and thus you will find her: frankness and friendship, assimilation of new things and old traditions, art and spontaniety, popular festivities and aristocratic elegance, solid cooking and fine wines. All these will you find nestling under the protecting outspread wings of the Archangel Rafael, Guardian of travellers, who welcomes you from the tower of the Mosque.

---

[1] A bullfight where novillos, bulls that are two to three years old, are used. [2] *Salmorejo* is a sauce made from water, vinegar, oil, salt and pepper.

PLAN OF THE MOSQUE

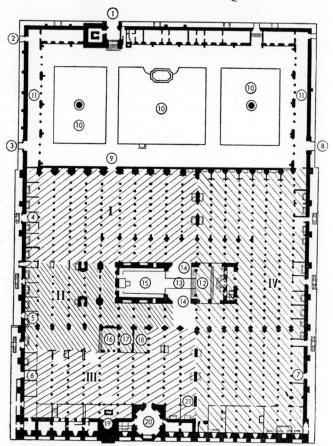

1. Gate of the Divine Pardon. — 2. Milk Wicket. — 3. Dean's Gate. — 4. St. Stephen's Gate. — 5. St. Michael's Gate. — 6. Palace Wicket. — 7. Wicket of the Ciborium. — 8 St. Catherine's Gate. — 9. Gate of the Palms. — 10. Courtyard of the Orange-trees. — 11. Cloister. — 12. High Altar. — 13. Transept. — 14. Pulpit. — 15. Choir. — 16. Villaviciosa Chapel. — 17. Chapel Royal. — 18. St. Paul's Chapel. — 19. Mihrab. — 20. St. Theresa's Chapel and Treasury. — 21. The Last Supper. — Spaces indicated: I: Naves of Abderrahman I. — II: Abderrahman II's amplification. — III: Alhaquen II's amplification. — IV: Naves of Almanzor.

Partial view of the town and bridge
over the Guadalquivir

House of the marquises of
Fuensanta del Valle

→
Calle de las Flores

House of the Fernández
de Mesa

Left: Calle Velázquez Bosco, former *calle de Comedias. Right, above: Plaza de la Compañía*. Church of Santa Victoria. *Below:* Altar of the *Virgen de los Faroles*

Above: W
front of
Mosque. S
Esteban D
Below: W
front of
Mosque. *P
tigo de*
lacio

Mosque
East fro

→

Mosque. The naves of
Almanzor

Mosque. Santa Cata-
lina Door

Mosque. *Puerta
del Perdón*

Mosque. Arches of the
Mihrab chapel

Left: Naves of Abderramán I.
Right, above: Villaviciosa
chapel. Detail of arches. *Below:* Mihrab. Interior

←
Cathedral. *Left:* pulpit. *Centre, above:*
«The Immaculate» by Damián de Castro. *Below:* «Saint Teresa», by José
de Mora

Cathedral nave and choir

Cathedral.
«The Last
Supper» by
Pablo de
Céspedes. *Below:* Detail
of the Cus-
tody of En-
rique de Arfe

Cathedr
Detail of
choir

The Mosque Tower seen from
the Patio of the Orange-Trees

← The Cathedral-Mosque, Door
of the Palms and Patio of
the Orange-Trees seen from
the Tower

Left, above: Statue of St.Raphael, Archangel, on the bridge over the Guadalquivir. *Below:* The *Calahorra. Right:* «The Triumph of St.Raphael» and the Bridge Gate

Church of San Francisco. «St.Andrew»
by Valdés Leal

Tower of the *Malmuerta*

Almodóvar Gate

→
Church of San Jacinto

Above: Church and
Tower of San Ni
colás de la Villa
Below: Plaza de la
Bulas

General Hospital. Chapel
of San Bartolomé

Casa de los Cea or *del
Indiano*. Window

Above: Iron gate of a Cordoban patio. *Below:* the patio of *El Zoco*

Left: Portillo Arch. Right, above: Moorish walls. Below: Plaza del Potro

Above: House of Jerónimo Páez, now the Archaeological Museum. *Below:* Patio of the house of the marquises of Carpio

Tower and gardens of the Alcázar Real

THREE TREASURES FROM THE PROVINCIAL ARCHAEOLOGICAL MUSEUM. *Above:* Bronze deer from Medina Azahara. *In the centre:* Germanic head. *Below:* A lion from New Carteia

Church of San Miguel.
Doorway

House of the Villalón

Patio de la Merced, now the Hospice

Left, above: Cuesta del Bailío.
Below: House of Don Gome
(Palace of the marquis of Via-
na). Garden. *Right:* Church of
San Lorenzo

Church of Santa Marina

La Fuenseca

Patio of the Fine Arts Museum

*On the next page: Plazuela de los
Dolores. «The Christ of the Lamps»*

HOTELS

DE LUXE CATEGORY

CÓRDOBA PALACE - Paseo de la Victoria
    Telephone 26380

FIRST CLASS A

SIMÓN - Gran Capitán, 9
    Telephone 21919

ZAHIRA - Conde Robledo, 1
    Telephone 26260

FIRST CLASS B

AVENIDA - Avenida Generalísimo, 28
    Telephone 23900

REGINA - Avenida Generalísimo, 25
    Telephone 21926

SECOND CLASS

ANDALUCÍA - José Zorrilla, 3
    Telephone 22147

CUATRO NACIONES - García Morato, 4
    Telephone 23925

EL BRILLANTE - Carretera del Brillante, 305 - Telephone 23940

GRANADA - Avenida América, 25
    Telephone 21864

VICTORIA - Plaza Aladreros, 13
    Telephone 21990

RESTAURANTS

DE LUXE CATEGORY

PLATA - Victoriano Rivera, 10
    Telephone 21724

FIRST CLASS

ALFONSO - Gondomar, 2
    Telephone 21325

EL BRILLANTE - Carretera del Brillante, 305 - Telephone 23940

CÍRCULO DE LA AMISTAD - Alfonso XII, 14 - Telephone 21880

CÍRCULO MERCANTIL - Gran Capitán, 2
    Telephone 23827

GRAN BAR - Plaza José Antonio
    Telephone 21036

GOL - Cuesta de la Pólvora, 2
    Telephone 23014

IMPERIO - Victoriano Rivera, 6
    Telephone 22452

LA HOSTERÍA - Sevilla, 2
    Telephone 21410

PARÍS - Cruz Conde - Telephone 24321

SAVARÍN - Gran Capitán, 13
    Telephone 24114

TYPICAL TAVERNS

CASA PEPE - Calle Romero, 1
    Telephone 22023

EL BOTERO - Alfaros, 6
    Telephone 21209

PRACTICAL INFORMATION SUPPLEMENT
TO THE GUIDE TO
CÓRDOBA

EL PISTO - Enmedio, 3
Telephone 24881

LOS CALIFAS - Deanes, 9
Telephone 23498

HOURS OF MEALS

Breakfast: from 8 a.m. to 10 a.m.

Lunch: from 12 a.m. to 16 p.m.

Dinner: from 20 p.m. to 23 p.m.

TEA ROOMS

DUNIA - Gran Capitán, 8
Telephone 22942

HISPANIA - Cruz Conde, 3
Telephone 22601

PARÍS - Cruz Conde - Telephone 24321

SANDÚA - Gran Capitán
Telephone 23097

BARS AND CAFES

AVENIDA - Avenida Generalísimo, 14
Telephone 24281

BENÍTEZ - Avenida Generalísimo
Telephone 23023

BOSTON - Plaza José Antonio
Telephone 22235

CAIRO - Sevilla, 5 and 7
Telephone 22302

COLONIAL - Morería, 1
Telephone 22794

CÓRDOBA - Victoriano Rivera, 4
Telephone 21377

GRAN BAR - Plaza José Antonio
Telephone 21036

IMPERIO - Victoriano Rivera, 6
Telephone 22452

FLORIDA - Concepción, 4
Telephone 22481

MIAMI - Marqués del Boil, 4
Telephone 22171

NEGRESCO - Victoriano Rivera, 14
Telephone 22735

PLATA - Victoriano Rivera, 8
Telephone 22588

PLAYA - Paseo de la Victoria
Telephone 23010

REMO - Cruz Conde

ROSALES - Avenida Generalísimo, s/n.
Telephone 22780

SODA FOUNTAINS

DAVID RICO - Jesús y María, 2
Telephone 21163

FLOR DE LEVANTE - Plaza de José Antonio, 3 - Telephone 24004

FLORIDA - Concepción, 4
Telephone 22481

ITALIANA - Concepción, 4

LA MEXICANA - Victoriano Rivera, 7
Telephone 22698

SÁNCHEZ - Gondomar, 14
Telephone 21640

THEATRES AND CINEMAS

ALCÁZAR - Reyes Católicos, 17
Telephone 21565

DUQUE DE RIVAS - Gran Capitán, 18
Telephone 21750

GÓNGORA - Jesús y María, 12
Telephone 22165

GRAN TEATRO - Gran Capitán, 3
Telephone 22700

PALACIO DEL CINE - Plaza de José
Antonio, 3 - Telephone 22174

CABARETS

EL OASIS - Córdoba Palace

KURSAAL ANDALUZ - Fiteros, 7
Telephone 21555

LA PRIMERA - Avenida América
Telephone 22873

LA SEGUNDA - Avenida América
Telephone 22253

EL ZOCO - Maimónides

BULLRING

PLAZA DE TOROS DE LOS TEJARES
Avenida Generalísimo, 36
Telephone 21043

SPORTS

PISCINA CÓRDOBA PALACE - Plaza de
la Victoria - Telephone 26380

PISCINA CIUDAD JARDÍN - Felipe II
Telephone 24332

ESTADIUM DEL ARCÁNGEL - Teresa Hoces - Telephone 23598

HANDICRAFTS

ADARVE LINARES - Torrijos, 8
Telephone 24274

HIJOS DE MANUEL FRAGERO - Avenida del Generalísimo, 14
Telephone 22406

LA CAMERANA - Claudio Marcelo, 23
Telephone 22000

PACREL - Cruz Conde, 8
Telephone 22371

BUSINESS HOURS

Winter: from 9 a.m. to 1 p.m. and
from 3 p.m. to 7 p.m.

Summer: from 9 a.m. to 1 p.m. and
from 4 p.m. to 8 p.m.

BANKS

BANCO DE BILBAO - Gran Capitán, 2
Telephone 23800

Banco Central - Gran Capitán, 11
Telephone 21900

Banco de España - Gran Capitán, 7
Telephone 21965

Banco Español de Crédito - Claudio
Marcelo, 21 - Telephone 21902

Banco Hipotecario - Claudio Marcelo, 17 - Telephone 22339

Banco Hipano Americano - Sevilla, 4
and 6 - Telephone 21924

Banco López e Hijos - Pedro López, 14 - Telephone 21226

Banco Rural y Mediterráneo
Gondomar, 12 - Telephone 23156

Banco de Santander - Gondomar, 3
Telephone 21942

Banco Vitalicio db España - Felipe II, 13 - Telephone 26521

Banco de Vizcaya - Concepción, 12
Telephone 21958

Banco Popular Español - Cruz Conde, 17 - Telephone 21226

Banco Popular Ibérico - Plaza José
Antonio

COMMUNICATIONS

General Post Office - Cruz Conde, 21 - Telephone 23327

Central Telegraph Office (Day and
nigh service) - Cruz Conde, 21
Telephone 22605

Telegrams by Phone (Teleben) - Call
number 23532

Central Telephone Exchange
Plaza de Cánovas - Telephone 03

TRANSPORTS

RAILWAYS

Renfe - Station: Avenida de América - Telephone 22890

Information service (tickets, timeta-
bles, reservations, etc): Avda. Generalísimo, 6 - Telephone 21648
Agenzie Office: Jesús y María, 1
Telephone 22414

BUSSES

Anónima Alsina - Gran Capitán, 12
Telephone 21738 (Busses to Cór-
doba-Seville and Córdoba-Granada)

TAXIS RANKS

Cardenal Herrero - Telephone 26127

Plaza de José Antonio
Telephone 22022

Avda. Gran Capitán - Telephone 22888

San Fernando - Telephone 26105

CARRIAGE RANK

Estación Central de los FF. CC.

Hotel Córdoba Palace

Hotel Regina

Calle Torrijos

GARAGES

Alcázar - Puerta del Rey
Telephone 24250

América - Avda. de América, 17
Telephone 23203

Andalucía - Vista Alegre, 6
Telephone 23094

Autocar - Avda. Antonio Maura, 3
Telephone 23444

Avenida - Medina Azahara, 7
Telephone 22272

Azahara - Medina Azahara, 37
Telephone 22351

Córdoba - Carretera de Sevilla Km 404
Telephone 25838

Córdoba Palace - Avda. de la República Argentina

Costan - Alhaken II, 1
Telephone 21214

Ford - Avda. América
Telephone 22735

Esperanza - Puerta Colodro, 4
Telephone 23898

Sport - Conde Robledo, 3
Telephone 22734

Fiat - Diego Serrano - T. 23097

Victoria - Gran Capitán, 23
Telephone 22074

Palace - M. Benzo, 6
Telephone 26814

San Cayetano - Pérez Muñoz, 14
Telephone 25228

San Ramón - Siete de Mayo, 7
Telephone 23973

OTHER DATES FOR INTEREST

Real Automóvil Club - Morería, 14
Telephone 21000

Moto Club - Avda. Generalísimo, 1
Telephone 24081

TO SEND PARCELS ABROAD

Transportes Internacionales - Federico Michel - Hernando Colón, 11-13 - Telephone 23213 - Sevilla

CONSULATES

Colombia - Maese Luis, 11
Telephone 22991

Mónaco - Málaga, 6
Telephone 24391

France - Aixa - Telephone 21213

Italy - Mármol de Bañuelos, 1
Telephone 25276

TRAVEL AGENCIES

American Express - Jesús y María, 1
Telephone 22424

VIAJES BAKUMAR - Jesús y María, 3
Telephone 22414

VIAJES BAIXAS - García Morato, 1
Telephone 21618

VIAJES MARSANS Jesús y María, 1
Telephone 22424

VIAJES MELIÁ - Córdoba Palace and
Morería, 7 - Telephone 24269

WAGONS/LITS-COOK - Hotel Regina
Telephone 21927

TOURIST INFORMATION OFFICE

DIRECCIÓN GENERAL DE TURISMO (Information Office) - Velázquez Bosco, 14 - Telephone 21054

OFICINA MUNICIPAL DE TURISMO
Judá Levi - Telephone 24099

MUSEUMS

ARCHEOLOGICAL MUSEUM - Velázquez Bosco, 7 - Telephone 24011 - Visiting hours: from 10 a.m. to 13 p.m. and from 15 p.m. to 18 p.m.

CATEDRALICIO - Mezquita-Catedral

JULIO ROMERO DE TORRES - Plaza del Potro - Telephone 21314 - Visiting hours: from 9.30 a.m. to 13.30 p.m. and from 15 p.m. to 18 p.m.

MUNICIPAL DE ARTE CORDOBÉS
Plaza de las Bulas
Telephone 25103

PROVINCIAL MUSEUM OF FINE ARTS
Plaza del Potro - Telephone 21314
Visiting hours: from 9.30 a.m. to 13.30 p.m. and from 15 p.m. to 18 p.m.

OFFICIAL CENTRES

TOWN HALL - Calvo Sotelo, 1
Telephone 21803

POLICE HEADQUARTERS - Gran Capitán, 18 - Telephone 22287

CIVIL GOVERNMENT - Gran Capitán, 18
Telephone 21066

BISHOPRIC - Torrijos, 10
Telephone 21434

LIBRARIES

SÉNECA - Jardines de Agricultura

PROVINCIAL - Calvo Sotelo (Palacio Diputación) - Visiting hours: *Winter:* from 17.30 p.m. to 20 p.m. *Summer:* from 9.30 a.m. to 14 p.m.

MUNICIPAL - Edificio Ayuntamiento

ISLÁMICA - Jardines Plaza de Colón

ANDAR Y VER Collection. Guides to Spain

Now Ready:

Majorca by Lorenzo Villalonga. **Iviza** by Arturo Llopis. **The "Costa Brava"** by Néstor Luján. **Barcelona** by «Jaime Miravall». **The Montserrat** by José María de Sagarra. **Valencia** by Martín Domínguez Barberá. **Madrid** by César González-Ruano. **Toledo** by Gaspar Gómez de la Serna. **The Escorial** by Luis Felipe Vivanco. **Avila** by Camilo José Cela. **Segovia** by the Marquis of Lozoya. **Salamanca** by Rafael Santos Torroella. **Burgos** by Fray Justo Pérez de Urbel. **Granada** by Francisco Prieto-Moreno. **Seville** by Rafael Laffón. **Córdoba** by Ricardo Molina. **Málaga** by José María Souvirón. **Corunna** by Carlos Martínez-Barbeito. **Santiago de Compostela** by Ramón Otero Pedrayo. **«Rías Bajas»** of Galicia by José María Castroviejo.

In preparation:

Saragossa by Luis Monreal. **Gran Canaria** by Carmen Laforet. **Tenerife** by Vicente Marrero. **The Basque Country** by Ignacio Aldecoa. **Tarragona** by Sebastián Juan Arbó.

ANDAR Y VER Collection. Aspects of Spain

Now Ready:

Bulls and Bullfighting by José Luis Acquaroni.
Andalusian Dances by José Manuel Caballero Bonald.

In preparation:

Cante Flamenco and Cante Jondo by Néstor Luján.

"ANDAR Y VER". GUIDES TO SPAIN do not accept any advertisements. All establishments mentioned are done so freely.